KT-118-830

PLANTS FOR THE

WATER
GARDEN

PETER THURMAN

TIGER BOOKS INTERNATIONAL

First published in Great Britain in 1994 by
PAVILION BOOKS LIMITED
London House, Great Eastern Wharf, Parkgate Road,
London SW11 4NQ

This edition published in 1998 by
Tiger Books International PLC, Twickenham, U.K.

Text © Peter Thurman 1994

Conceived, edited and designed by Russell Ash & Bernard Higton
Picture research by Julia Pashley
Plant consultant Tony Lord

The moral right of the author has been asserted.

A CIP catalogue record for this book is available from
the British Library.

ISBN 1 85501 992 2

Printed in China by Sun Fung Offset Binding Co.
Produced in association with The Hanway Press Ltd., London

2 4 6 8 10 9 7 5 3 1

CONTENTS

....

INTRODUCTION

WATER IN THE GARDEN

....

Water is a clear, neutral, colourless, tasteless and odourless liquid that is essential for plant and animal life. It is one of the most important substances on the planet.

Early nomadic tribes stopped and settled near water and became farmers. Its availability meant that crops could be irrigated and livestock reared. Washing and sanitation – essential requirements for a stable and civilized society were made possible by water.

The aesthetic qualities of water – the sound of it on the move, its reflective qualities and the beauty of the fish and plants that are associated with it have long been appreciated. Water has been an integral part of gardens as long as there have been gardens – especially in hotter countries – where the importance of water as a life-giving force has always been respected. In a harsh, blazing climate, water allows trees to grow that in turn give shelter from the sun. The cooling combination of shade and water provides sanctuary and refuge, a desert oasis, a paradise garden.

Water has become an increasingly important element in garden design. In the domestic garden, the interest in wildlife, the desire to grow the many varieties of water plants or keep ornamental fish have turned into almost obsessive hobbies for some gardeners and interest in the water garden has never been greater.

OPPOSITE TOP: STOURHEAD, A CLASSIC EXAMPLE OF WATER IN AN ENGLISH LANDSCAPE GARDEN.
BOTTOM: COOLING WATER ARCHES IN THE ALHAMBRA, SPAIN.

THE GEOMETRIC APPROACH TO WATER IN THE GARDEN.

BASIC PRINCIPLES

The size and scale of your pond is a very important consideration. It must 'fit' the surrounding space and not overpower the rest of the garden, nor should it be too small and tucked away in a corner.

The permutations for a water garden are endless. Perhaps the fundamental choice is between a formal or informal feature. A formal pond should be geometric in shape – a perfect circle or square for example, with clearly defined, definite edges. Fish and fountains may be included, but an over-abundance of plants, except water-lilies perhaps, and other wildlife is less appropriate.

Some formal water features are deliberately completely devoid of plant and animal life. The textural and reflective qualities of the water and the sound of it on the move are all that is desired. Such water gardens make a dramatic architectural statement providing the garden with structure rather than decoration. Their restrained starkness is the attraction, emanating calmness and tranquillity and often providing the climax or centrepiece to a formal garden.

THE RELAXED STYLE OF THE INFORMAL POND.

Informal ponds can be looser in design and shape and perhaps combined with a rock garden and waterfall. The edges are deliberately vague and softened by bog and marginal plants. Wildlife of all kinds is positively encouraged by the creation of breeding sites and shelter. Informal water features are full of animal and plant interest all year round, creating a romantic and stimulating atmosphere.

Apart from the totally lifeless formal pond, all other water gardens need to be planned, located and maintained with one major factor in mind: ecological balance. Any water feature that includes living organisms (animals and/or plants) must be treated as a self-contained micro-habitat that is constantly changing but continually striving to reach or maintain a biological equilibrium. Submerged aquatic plants are essential to mop up some of the nutrients, oxygenate the water and to provide good shelter for wildlife.

If a water garden is properly designed, built and stocked, it will eventually 'settle down' and look after itself. All the surprises will then be pleasant ones and plagues of gnats, algification, blocked pump filters, invasive plant species and leaks will be avoided.

A water garden feature must be safe. The electricity supply for water pumps, lighting, and pond heaters must be properly installed and the potential dangers of water to toddlers must be given very careful consideration.

BOLD DRIFTS OF PLANTS AT THE WATER'S EDGE.

CREATING A WATER GARDEN

Location

Having decided you would like a water feature or pond it is important to select the best position. Most bog and aquatic plants need at least some sun to grow and flower well. Four hours per day is an acceptable minimum for most, although water-lilies prefer more and some foliage bog plants will tolerate less. Not only will nearby or overhanging trees and shrubs reduce light levels but also fallen leaves and their roots can cause problems. Decaying leaves in a pond give off toxic gases that are harmful to fish and other water life and the all-important ecological balance is disrupted. Tree and shrub roots may make pond excavations difficult and later cause damage to the completed pond.

Avoid areas that are regularly fertilized, such as those near a vegetable plot or immaculate lawn. Wind and rain may carry the nutrients into the water, leading to a build-up of algae – again adversely affecting the 'balance'. A wildlife pond should be located in a peaceful spot. Even quite shy creatures will take up residence if they find a quiet refuge and a safe breeding ground.

Pond Construction

There are various methods of constructing a pond:

Puddling

This is the traditional method of creating a pond and involves smearing clay into a watertight seal. It is obviously worth trying it if you have a clay soil, alternatively clay can be purchased in a dried bag form known as Bentonite.

In times past, the pond was excavated and teams of horses would be used to drag a mat up and down to smear the clay. The seal would be built up in layers using straw or other locally available materials to help bind up the clay. Today it is all done by machinery. This is an excellent method for very large areas of water or where the water table is naturally high, and is especially suitable for a wildlife pond. Being labour intensive it can still prove to be expensive. In dry seasons there is always a danger of the clay cracking and the seal being broken. It is a messy job requiring a lot of skill but is still carried out by craftsmen and specialized firms in rural areas where appropriate.

Concrete

This involves the construction of a concrete floor and walls or sides to the pond. Having excavated the hole (larger than required to compensate for the concrete), a 15 cm thick layer of hard-core base must be laid down which is then blinded with sand. Ten to 15 cm of concrete (8:1 cement/ballast mix) with a waterproofing agent mixed in is then spread over the base – perhaps reinforced with metal rods or mesh.

The sides are constructed by using timber shuttering to

contain the concrete that is poured in and tamped down a section at a time. Vertical sides will need shuttering on both sides. On sloping sides the soil is blinded with sand before the concrete is poured in. The edges or rim of a concrete pond should ideally be thicker as this is where the most pressure is exerted when the pool is iced over. The top edge can be finished off with paving or brickwork or designed to contain shelves or pockets for soil to provide a shallow water area for marginal plants. This is more satisfactory than propping plant containers up with bricks.

Concrete pools should last for many years – especially if constructed well and all in one go rather than in separate phases on different days. Concrete pools can however leak in time, particularly with soil subsidence or after a severe winter when a thick layer of ice on top of the water expands with such force that it can stress or crack the pond's sides. The latter is easily avoided by maintaining holes in the ice to allow for expansion. This can be achieved by floating objects on the water (perhaps a football) or gently and carefully melting the ice with boiling water. Never violently smash the ice – the shock waves can harm or even kill fish. Sloping sides (30°) are also preferable to vertical sides (although not so desirable in formal designs), as they allow ice formation to ride upwards thus greatly reducing the pressure on the walls.

When fresh, concrete releases toxic levels of lime into the water. You need to wait for three to four months before stocking the pond with plants and fish or alternatively seal the concrete with a neutralizing and water-proofing paint. Once the concrete has set, it may be rendered to a thickness of 2 cm using a sharp-sand and cement (3:1) mix, again adding a waterproofing agent. Even then it may be advisable to fill the pond with water and leave for a few days to absorb the worst of the chemicals from the concrete or rendering before pumping out and re-filling.

PRE-FABRICATED OR PRE-FORMED PONDS

These are made of rigid, durable plastic or reinforced fibre-glass moulded into various set shapes. The thinner, cheaper types are weaker and prone to physical damage or, in time, degradation by ultra-violet light from the sun. As with most products, you get what you pay for.

The hole should be excavated and then lined with sand or wet newspaper to act as a soft buffer between the soil and the pre-cast shell. First impressions of this method can be misleading as it is not as simple as it looks. It is difficult to get the level exactly right and the mould, to look natural, must be perfectly horizontal. A spirit-level and the addition of some water into the pond to encourage settlement helps but it can involve a lot of 'fine tuning' and ramming more sand into any gaps. This is especially difficult under planting shelves or the shell base. Forcing sand into awkward cavities with a jet of water from a hosepipe may help.

The drawbacks of these rigid pond liners are the limited range of shape options and restriction in size. In addition, most have steep sides (incorporating ledges for plants) which make them less than ideal for a wildlife pond. The top edges are also well defined. This makes them difficult to mask except by turf, stone or slabs which may not be desirable. In a nutshell, these pre-formed liners are best used when a small, relatively cheap formal pond is required.

Flexible pond liners

Made from PVC or butyl rubber, these liners are perhaps the most versatile pond-making materials, suitable for most styles and sizes of water features. They are flimsy yet strong and elastic enough to tolerate stretching and uneven or contoured pond outlines. To calculate the size of pond liner required, calculate the total top surface area of the pond and multiply this figure by twice the maximum depth.

Having excavated the hole, remove any sharp stones or

objects and then cover the soil with a 20 to 40 cm layer of sand or old pieces of carpet to prevent puncturing. Then position the liner, allowing for a decent overlap all the way round the edge. Weigh down the edges of the liner with bricks or slabs and then pour the water in. The weight of the water forces the liner to take the shape of the hole – whether it be simple and formal or natural and intricately complex. To avoid wasteful pleats and tucks, however, informal ponds should have bold sweeping contours rather than sudden and sharp changes in direction. Trim off any excess material around the edges leaving about 30 to 40 cm to tuck in under the surrounding soil and/or mask with rocks or turf. Boggy areas can be easily created by extending the liner into a shallow depression.

Flexible liners can then be completely hidden by a layer of soil, especially if the sides are very gently sloping. This also makes marginal and bog planting easy and avoids the use of containers, which is especially desirable in an informal or wildlife pond.

Do not be tempted to use polythene. It is very cheap but may split when stretched or at best will only last a few years, becoming brittle under sunlight. PVC liners are stronger and more durable but will still last for only five to 10 years.

Although more expensive, butyl rubber liners which are guaranteed for over twenty years are more cost effective in the long term. Holes in butyl liners can be cheaply repaired with a simple puncture repair kit – but it will mean that you have to empty or partially empty the pond to get at it. For large ponds or even lakes, sheets of butyl rubber can be very successfully heat-bonded together on site. All in all, butyl liners are probably the best option for the widest range of water-garden features.

One word of warning regarding flexible liners: make sure that the excavated hole is clear of decaying vegetable matter before positioning the liner. If the methane gas given off

Excavating the hole with 'shelves' for planting.

Placing the liner over the hole and stabilizing with stones.

Filling the pond.

Masking the exposed edge of the liner with suitable materials.

SIMPLIFIED STEP-BY-STEP GUIDE TO CREATING A POND WITH A FLEXIBLE LINER.

13

A WATER FEATURE SUITABLE FOR EVEN THE SMALLEST GARDEN.

cannot escape through the soil or around the edge of the liner it will cause the liner to balloon up in the centre of the pond.

Small water gardens
Remember that anything watertight can be used to create a water feature. In a small garden or on a patio you can use an old sink, half oak barrels or even an old bath or cattle trough sunk into the ground or left above ground and surrounded by cobbles or rocks. Even the smallest of ponds can be planted up with dwarf and slow-growing plants and provide a habitat for a wide range of aquatic animals that will provide lots of interest to children.

WATER GARDEN DETAILS

Moving Water
Still water is peaceful and calm and the reflective qualities are maximized. The sight and musical sound of water on the move on the other hand, whether it be a soothing trickle or an exciting, vibrant gushing, adds another dimension to the garden and provides a unique atmosphere.

In a self-contained, otherwise still, body of water, the water must be re-circulated by an electric pump. Water can be pumped between ponds at different levels over a waterfall or babbling brook or quite simply through a fountain or other water spouting mechanism.

The advantages are great – oxygen levels in the water are raised, which benefits fish and the general well being of your pond, dust and debris are less likely to settle as a surface scum and the growth of green algae is inhibited. The disadvantages are that moving water is usually colder than still water – which is fine in summer but less desirable in winter. Some plants (especially water-lilies) dislike disturbed water and growth and flowering may be affected.

Pumps
There are two basic types of pump: submersible and surface. Submersible pumps, as the name suggests, operate under water. They are relatively cheap to buy and easy to install. They are equipped with a water filter to protect the motor and are very quiet. The pond keeps the pump cool. Any fountain or spout attachment is connected directly to the pump or via a length of hosepipe. For a waterfall or similar feature, the water has to be moved from one level to another. The pump is placed in the lowest part and the water is pumped via a hosepipe back up to the top level. Gravity does the rest. Try to make sure that the components of such a system are completely hidden.

There are different sizes of pumps with varying capacities normally measured in litres/hr output (1,000 to 15,000 litres/hr is the normal range). This, along with the diameter and length of hosepipe and the height difference between the pump and the outlet, will determine the actual water flow rate. It is important to check that the pump you choose is capable of doing the job. It is better to go for the next powerful model up rather than buy one that will constantly struggle to recycle the water at the required rate. Submersible pumps are suitable for most domestic water gardens that are small to medium in size.

Surface pumps are more expensive but much more powerful and are situated out of water. They are more difficult and costly to install as they involve 'proper' plumbing, but have a much greater capacity for larger waterfalls or where a series of fountains or cascades are required. Surface pumps need priming, and they are noisy. They are usually housed in some form of sound- and weather-proofed shelter or underground chamber. Being above water however, means that they are easier to maintain. Surface pumps need be considered only for large-scale water gardens that involve a large or spectacular water display. Some models are capable of over 30,000 litres/hr output.

Fountains and spouting ornaments
Fountain nozzles are available in a variety of forms that determine the water pattern. A fountain can be a bell-shaped curtain of water, a small, gurgling cascade or a fine jet spray lifted several metres into the air.

Fountains can also be incorporated into free-standing statues or architectural mouldings, even wall-mounted features that spout water, such as a lion's head or decorative tap, are available and are suitable for even a small courtyard garden.

A very small moving water feature can be created by simply pumping water through the central hole in a millstone so that it bubbles out over the stone surface and then falls down the sides for recycling. Various sizes of mill stones are now being purpose-built for this use.

In draughty areas or small areas of water, beware of spray drift from a fountain. This can be a nuisance, quickly reducing water levels so that they constantly need to be replenished.

A SPOUTING ARCHITECTURAL DETAIL PROVIDES PERPETUAL INTEREST.

When selecting a fountain for your pond, try to keep it in scale. A small gurgle will be lost in a lake and a giant geyser would be ridiculous in a small town garden.

Waterfalls and cascades
In the informal water garden, waterfalls and cascades are often incorporated into a rock garden. In a more formal setting it may be just a question of positioning interconnected pools of water at different levels and a pump will do the rest.

If you are lucky enough to have a natural stream or spring in your garden, then damming the supply into pools will automatically create a series of interconnecting waterfalls – but consult your regional office of the National Rivers Authority before you alter a watercourse in any way. In most gardens, however, waterfalls and cascades are created by re-circulating a given volume of water by means of a pump.

It is important to remember that such a feature, natural or constructed, must be watertight and effectively treated as part of the pond. The moving water area of a feature, whether it be over rocks or down a gully, needs to be completely sealed using the same basic materials that are available to construct the pool itself. Through a rockery, the waterfall area needs to be sealed with a waterproof cement, perhaps with a colour additive to help blend in with the rocks. Alternatively, a flexible liner can be used to define the water course which is then masked by the rocks and scree. There are also pre-formed, moulded waterfall sections available in a variety of shapes and sizes but they are restrictive and it is difficult to hide the fact that they are plastic.

Lighting
Unlike many garden design 'innovations', lighting is a totally 20th-century development. All parts of a garden can now be lit but it is perhaps the water garden that is most

successful and spectacular. Pools, cascades and especially
fountains, where each droplet becomes a shining pearl when
illuminated, as well as the surrounding plants, take on a
different character at night.

Waterproof electric lights can be floated on the water
surface or submerged by weights. Alternatively they can be
mounted on movable spikes that are pushed into the water
margins or bank. The lights can be flood or spot types. The
flood will illuminate a wide area, whereas the spot throws a
concentrated beam on to a feature, which gives a more
dramatic effect. Lamps are available in various colours but
clear, white light is perhaps the most satisfactory.

SAFETY

Electricity
Water and electricity are uneasy bedfellows. The electricity
supply to a pond should be installed by a qualified electri-
cian. Special care must be taken to ensure that the whole
system is insulated and watertight. Cables should be
armoured and, in a border, buried deeper than normal
digging will reach. Keep a plan showing the routes of any
underground services, which will be useful to you and
future occupiers. Some pumps can work through a trans-
former to a lower AC voltage or very low DC voltage. All
outside mains circuits should be fitted with a circuit breaker.
It can be wired into the fuse box or be part of a socket or
plug.

Children
A baby or toddler can drown in just a few inches of water.
The number of drownings in domestic ponds per year is
alarmingly high. A pond should be securely fenced off at all
times if there is a risk that that your own or visiting children
could gain unsupervised access to water.

STOCKING YOUR POND

Animals and Insects

Very soon after you have filled your pond with water, nature will stock it with a teeming variety of creatures. Many are invisible to the naked eye but all have a part to play in the balanced pond community. Water is like a magnet to wildlife and soon your pond will be full of everything from frogs and newts to snails, beetles and a myriad other insects. Above the water the air and water plants act as a breeding ground for dragon and damselflies – all fascinating to watch.

Fish

Fish are not essential, but to many water gardeners they are the main reason for having a pond. Many water plants pests and the larvae of gnats and mosquitoes that are attracted to still water are eaten by fish, while fish excreta, which is rich in nutrients, will feed your pond plants.

Choose fish carefully: carp, tench and rudd spend most of their time at the bottom, so you never see them and the water will always be agitated and muddy unless the pond floor is covered with a layer of stones or gravel. The easiest decorative fish are goldfish and their many varieties such as shubunkins and golden orfe. The aristocrats of hardy pond fish are the Japanese koi carp. In larger ponds these can reach quite a size and they have become a very popular hobby. Many aquatic centres sell a wide range of fish at prices to suit all budgets. Koi, revered by the Japanese for centuries, can change hands for astronomical prices: large exhibition specimens are worth tens of thousands of pounds.

Brightly coloured fish are most vulnerable to predators such as herons. Water plants provide some protection but to prevent losses completely or to an acceptable level (especially if you have valuable koi) a permanent cover of netting may be necessary. If you live in a cold district where winter

WATER LILIES PROVIDING SHADE FOR ORNAMENTAL FISH.

temperatures are likely to be consistently below zero, a cover for the pond and a heater are advisable. These will not only protect your fish but also prevent ice damage to certain types of pond, such as those made of concrete.

Fish will also eat frog spawn and too many in a relatively small pond can upset the balance of nature. If you want an interesting wildlife pond it is best not to stock it with fish. Small natives such as sticklebacks or minnows may appear as if by magic (the eggs are carried on the legs of birds) and a few of these are acceptable.

Plants
Plants suitable for the water garden are usually categorized by their growth habit and requirements into the following groups.

• Water's edge plants
• Bog or shallow marginal plants
• Deep marginal plants
• Floating and deep water aquatics
• Oxygenating, submerged aquatics.

Water's edge plants
These are any plants – trees, shrubs and perennials – that tolerate or prefer the moist conditions often found by the side of the water. Some will even cope with periods of flooding, but most prefer to have their roots above the waterline for most of the time. The habit, outline and colour of these plants needs to be considered because they are often the largest or most dominant species near water and their reflection in the water gives you two plants for the price of one.

Bog or shallow marginal plants
A bog garden is a marshy area of ground which rarely dries out but is never permanently water-logged nor has water deeper than five centimetres for any length of time. Many herbaceous plants and grasses are especially suited to this type of habitat. Such areas are both naturally and artificially associated with water gardens. The junction between the water garden and *terra firma* is an important habitat for many forms of wildlife (especially reptiles and amphibians). The plants that grow in these areas not only provide shelter and protection for such animals but also help mask the edges of constructed, artificial water gardens and the materials that were used. They are normally planted directly into the soil.

A SEQUENCE OF STONE BRIDGE PATHWAYS ACROSS A CASCADING STREAM.

Deep marginal plants
These are plants that prefer their roots almost permanently submerged in water but have leaves and flowers that grow above the water line. Some are very decorative and afford shelter for pond wildlife. Plant either directly into the soil or, in deeper ponds, in baskets or other types of container placed on shelves, ledges or stacked up on bricks. Like all aquatic plants plunged in containers, use a clay loam rooting medium and cover the surface with shingle to try to reduce the amount of soil released into the water. Some pieces of charcoal will help keep the soil 'sweet'. To feed container-

ized plants with minimal effect on the water, mix some bonemeal with wet clay, form it into a ball shape and push into the surface of the basket. Alternatively use a special pond plant fertilizer which quickly breaks down.

Floating or deep water aquatics
The leaves of these plants float on the surface of the water but the roots require permanent deep water. They are best grown in baskets of soil, raised up to the right level. This allows the plant to be lifted out of the water for thinning, dividing or feeding. In large or natural ponds this may not be practical. Here, floating aquatics are best allowed to grow into the soil on the pond or lake bottom.

Water-lilies, probably the most decorative and highly prized of all aquatic plants come under this category. Large leaf floating aquatics such as water-lilies provide shade and cover for fish and other pond life and a basking platform for frogs.

Many floating aquatics such as *azolla*, have free, water-borne root systems. As they are natives of the tropics, they are often tender in northern temperate regions and may be killed off in winter.

Oxygenating, submerged aquatics
These are vital for an ecologically balanced pond. They are usually inconspicuous underwater plants that release oxygen directly into the water. On a warm sunny day you can actually see the bubbles. Fish and plants use up oxygen and it is these plants that help replace it. By taking up mineral salts from the water they also reduce algal growth. As a result, they keep the water clear and provide shelter for spawning fish and their fry. They are normally 'planted' by simply throwing a few sprigs into the pond, perhaps attached to a weight to keep them under water. Select your oxygenating plants carefully (see Directory) some are far too invasive and vigorous for smaller pond.

PLANTS DIRECTORY

The following plants are all suitable for the
various positions associated with water gardens.

Plants are listed in alphabetical order of Latin name
followed by the common name, if any. The common name is
excluded if it is identical to the Latin name.

The 'fact line' shows, in order:

Size – height in metres (excluding surface-lying plants) and spread in
metres of a mature plant (where applicable).

Plant type

E Water's edge plant tolerating moist conditions.

B Bog or shallow marginal plant (0 to 5 cm)

M Deep marginal plant (5 to 30 cm)

F Floating or deep water aquatic

O Oxygenating, submerged aquatic

Site – tolerances, preferences or special requirements

ACORUS CALAMUS SWEET FLAG
A semi-evergreen perennial rush with iris-like leaves. When crushed, the leaves release a strong cinnamon scent used in days gone by for strewing floors to mask unpleasant smells. The flowers are inconspicuous but there is an attractive variegated-leaved variety. (*A. c.* 'Variegatus'). *A. gramineus* is a smaller (0.3 m) evergreen species. 'Ogon' has gold bands that are particularly bright in winter.

0.9 × 0.5   B   Sun or part shade

ALNUS
A. glutinosa is our native alder, a medium to large deciduous tree with rounded leaves, craggy bark and attractive yellow-green catkins in spring. It is eventually a large tree, suitable only for the edges of large ponds or lakes. *A.g.* 'Imperialis' and 'Laciniata' are small- to medium-sized trees with gracefully cut or divided leaves. Other species of alder are equally at home in damp conditions. *A. cordata*, the Italian alder, with dark green glistening leaves, is particularly attractive.

20.0 × 6.0   E   Sun or shade

APONOGETON DISTACHYOS CAPE PONDWEED, WATER HAWTHORN
A deciduous perennial with floating, oblong leaves and very fragrant, white, branched flowers that appear amongst the foliage intermittently throughout the summer. It will thrive in even quite shallow ponds.

0.10 × 1.2   F   Sun

ARUM ITALICUM LORDS AND LADIES
Tuberous perennial that produces leaves in autumn that last through winter. The greenish-white flowers appear in spring and comprise an attractive vertical spathe that encloses a columnar, pencil-like spadix. It likes a moist but not boggy soil. In late summer a cluster of orange-red berries appears on

Aponogeton distachyos

a stout stalk. *A. italicum* subsp. *italicum* (syn. *A.i.* 'Pictum') has narrow spear-shaped leaves that are marbled with grey and cream.

0.5 × 0.3   E   Sun or partial shade

ARUNCUS DIOICUS GOAT'S BEARD

This is a much undervalued perennial of shrub-like proportions, with handsome fern-like foliage and, in summer, plumes of creamy white flowers. It will actually grow in any soil but is especially attractive near the water's edge. *A.d.* 'Kneiffii' is a smaller version (0.9 m tall) with finer foliage.

1.8 × 1.2   E   Sun or shade

ASTILBE

One of the showiest of all waterside perennials. The tapering spikes of brightly coloured flowers appear throughout summer. Very hardy and never requiring support, they like it wet but dislike complete flooding for anything more than a few days. The foliage is daintily divided and often tinted. *A. × arendsii* is the name given to the main group of hybrids

27

which have white, pink, red or magenta flowers. *A. chinensis* is a fine species with a dwarf variety, *pumila,* that is a creeping, ground cover plant. *A.c.* var. *taquetii* has purple flowers in late summer when most astilbes have finished. All in all astilbes are very good value plants. The huge range of named varieties demands further investigation before selection. One word of warning: some varieties have very strong, insistent flower colours that must be carefully positioned so as not to kill other colours nearby. Often they look better en masse in splendid isolation.

0.6 to 1.0 × 0.6 to 0.8   E or B   Sun or part shade

AZOLLA CAROLINIANA FAIRY MOSS, WATER FERN
A very strange plant, this: it is a true water fern, deciduous and perennial, with small divided fronds that float on the surface. In full sun or colder weather they are tinged pink or purple, in shade, green to blue-green; either way a smooth, floating carpet of colour. The blue tints are caused by the presence of a blue-green algae which fixes nitrogen for the *Azolla* which, in return, shelters the algae. The fronds are virtually non-wettable and, if prodded underwater, immediately bob up again completely devoid of water droplets. It can be too invasive for the smallest of ponds, but being tender is often killed back in a harsh winter. To be safe, over-winter a small clump in a pan placed in a frost-free place. The shade *Azolla* creates also reduces the development of green algae.

0.05 × 1.0 to 2.0   F   Sun or part shade

BUTOMUS UMBELLATUS FLOWERING RUSH
Deciduous perennial with rush-like leaves, hence the common name. Beautiful umbels of delicate pink to rose-red flowers are produced in summer. It loves the sludgy edges of ponds.

1.0 × 0.5   B or M   Sun

Arum italicum subsp. *italicum*

Arunculus dioicus

Astilbe

Butomus umbellatus

CALTHA PALUSTRIS MARSH MARIGOLD, KINGCUP

A beautiful, undemanding British native with rounded, dark-green leaves and shiny yellow buttercup flowers that appear in spring. A larger, earlier-flowering and more rampant variety is sold as *C. polypetala*.

C. p. var. *alba* – white, long-lasting flowers.

C. p. 'Flore Pleno' – a showy double variety.

0.6 × 0.5   B or M   Sun or part shade

CAREX SEDGE

A diverse group of grasses that all tolerate or prefer moist conditions. The following are readily available and the pick of the bunch:

C. elata 'Aurea' – Bowles' golden sedge, an evergreen, tufted perennial with bright golden-yellow leaves. (0.4 × 0.3).

C. hachijoensis 'Evergold' – a dwarf and colourful sedge (0.2 × 0.3) with yellow-striped arching leaves; prefers some shade.

C. pendula – pendulous sedge, evergreen with a graceful arching habit and pendant flowers in summer; suitable for larger ponds, especially in shady quarters.

C. riparia – the greater pond sedge, tall and upright British

Carex elata 'Aura'

Caltha palustris   *Cornus alba* 'Sibirica'

native suitable for lakes. *C. r.* 'Variegata' has white striped leaves and is both elegant and invasive.

0.2 to 1.2 × 0.3 to 0.9   E or B   Sun or shade

CERATOPHYLLUM DEMERSUM HORNWORT
A submerged, occasionally floating, deciduous perennial with dark green feathery foliage. It grows in dense masses which provide shelter for many pond creatures including snails and insects. The plant is brittle and easily controlled by breaking up and lifting out. This fragmenting characteristic is also the method by which it spreads.

– × 1.0 to 2.0 m   O   Sunny but cool water

CORNUS DOGWOOD
A large group of deciduous shrubs or small trees. The following shrubby types are excellent for waterside locations around medium to large ponds:
C. alba, the red-barked dogwood – a thicket of red leafless stems in winter.

C. a. 'Elegantissima' – white variegated leaves.

C. a. 'Sibirica' – brilliant crimson young stems that are produced annually by hard cutting back in spring.

C. a. 'Spaethii' – yellow variegated leaves.

C. sanguinea – our native dogwood, with dark red stems and rich purple autumn foliage.

C. stolonifera 'Flaviramea' – yellow to olive-green stems.

1.5 × 1.5   E   Sun or part shade

DARMERA PELTATA UMBRELLA PLANT

A giant saxifrage with rounded heads of starry-pink flowers on long stems in spring before the leaves appear. They follow soon after and are large and rounded with the stalk connected to their centres – hence the common name. The creeping root system helps bind the soil and prevent erosion. *Darmera* is a newish name and the plant is still listed by many nurseries under its former name, *Peltiphyllum peltatum*. *D. p.* 'Nana' is a fine dwarf for the smaller pond with good autumn foliage tints.

Darmera peltata

1.0 × 0.6   E or B   Sun or shade

DICENTRA BLEEDING HEART

A beautiful group of herbaceous perennials that appreciate the cool, moist, dappled shade so often found on the edges of water. The common name describes the pendant heart or locket-shaped flowers that can be red, white, pink or yellow.

D. formosa – pretty fern-like foliage and deep pink flowers in late spring. There are some excellent varieties such as:

'Langtrees' – glaucous foliage and white flowers.

'Stuart Boothman' – as 'Langtrees', but more divided foliage and pink flowers.

'Luxuriant' – dark pink to crimson flowers.

Dicenta spectabilis

Euphorbia palustris

D. spectabilis – larger, with arching stems of rosy-red pendant hearts in spring; 'Alba' is a good white-flowered variety.

0.3 to 0.6 × 0.3 to 0.6   E   Cool sun or part shade

....

EICHHORNIA CRASSIPES WATER HYACINTH
A strange, tender perennial plant that is able to float due to its air-filled swollen leaf bases. The lilac flower spikes do not appear outdoors in the UK, but the plant's curious structure provides interest in summer, especially for children. It will be killed by the first frosts. This and the water lettuce (*Pistia stratiotes*) which has hairy, lettuce-like leaves are best described and treated as aquatic bedding plants. In the tropics, *Eichhornia* is a serious water weed able to block even the widest of waterways.

0.2 × 0.3   F   Sun

....

EUPHORBIA PALUSTRIS SPURGE
A spectacular clump-forming spurge producing large heads of bright yellow-green flowers in late spring. It revels in damp soils but will also grow well on drier sites.

0.9 × 0.9   E   Sun or part shade

....

FILIPENDULA MEADOWSWEET
Herbaceous perennials with flat, feathery heads of tiny flowers in summer. The following are the best for a water-side position:
F. palmata – handsome leaves on tall stems (1.2 m) and pink flowers; try to seek out 'Elgantissima' which has a deeper pink flower colour.
F. purpurea – large leaves forming big clumps and tiny cerise-crimson flowers; it prefers some shade.
F. ulmaria – our native meadowsweet with white flowers, ideal for the edges of a wildlife pond.
'Aurea' – a decorative, yellow-leaved form.
'Variegata' – leaves splashed with yellow.

0.6 to 1.2 × 0.5   E or B   Sun or shade

....

Filipendula purpurea   *Fritillaria meleagris*

FRITILLARIA MELEAGRIS SNAKE'S-HEAD FRITILLARY

An extraordinary bulbous perennial with narrow, greyish leaves and pendant bell-like flowers that have a distinctly chequered, pale and dark-pink pattern. It has such an exotic appearance it is hard to believe it is a British native of the wet meadows from the west country to East Anglia (although some botanists do dispute this). It readily seeds itself around, quickly colonizing moist grassy areas, always with the white flowered albino form present as well. In the wild it is very rare and protected, but nursery-grown plants or bulbs are readily available.

0.3 × 0.1   E   Sun

GENTIANA ASCLEPIADEA WILLOW GENTIAN

This perennial is far removed from the popular conception of a gentian, considered by many to be a dwarf alpine, that needs a well drained, preferably acidic soil and full sun. The willow gentian is tall, prefers moist shade and tolerates chalky soils. It

Gentiana asclepiadea

Glyceria maxima var. *variegata*

Gunnera manicata

has willow-like leaves (hence the common name) on arching stems that in early autumn bear pairs of pure blue gentian flowers. 'Knightshayes' is taller with flowers with a pale throat.

0.8 × 0.6   E   Part or full shade

....

GLYCERIA MAXIMA   REED SWEET GRASS

A thuggish perennial grass requiring plenty of room so that it can spread freely. It can be a problem even on dry soils. On the edges of large ponds or lakes the invasive roots become an advantage – quickly colonizing and stabilizing banks and providing cover for wildlife. It is normally seen in its variegated variety (*G. m.* var. *variegata*) which has creamy-yellow stripes that are tinged red at the beginning and end of the growing season.

1.0 × 1.5   E or B   Sun or shade

....

GUNNERA MANICATA   PRICKLY RHUBARB

A massive herbaceous perennial with strange green flower spikes half a metre long and leaves up to two metres in diameter, it looks as though its has escaped from the pages of *The Day of the Triffids*! Protect the crowns in winter with bracken, feed with copious amounts of well-rotted manure, and plant only around large ponds or lakes.

G. chilensis – similar but smaller, and so suitable for medium-sized ponds.

G. magellanica – an incredible miniature mat-forming species reaching only a few centimetres in height and spread.

2.0 × 3.0   E or B   Sun and part shade

....

HOSTA   PLANTAIN LILY, GIBOSHI

A large group of highly decorative perennials with arching leaves and lily-like flowers. The range of leaf sizes, shapes and colours is enormous and the plants themselves can be small and dainty right up to large bulging clumps. Although they prefer shade they will grow in sun as long as the soil keeps

moist. You will find *H. crispula, H. fortunei, H. undulata* and
H. sieboldiana and their forms readily available and at a reasonable price. Some of the choice or newer varieties are obtainable only from specialist growers and at a high price.

0.3 to 1.0 × 0.4 to 1.0   E   Shade or some sun

HOTTONIA PALUSTRIS WATER VIOLET
A perennial with dense whorls of deeply divided, submerged foliage. In summer, spikes of beautiful primula-like pale lilac flowers appear above the water surface. These and other submerged aquatics are 'planted' in the water by simply throwing them in.

– × 1.5   O   Sun

HOUTTUYNIA CORDATA
A creeping perennial with heart-shaped, orange-scented leaves and small white flowers that have green conical centres in summer. In autumn the foliage is tinted. The spreading habit can be too invasive for smaller water gardens.
'Chameleon' – a popular variety with variegated leaves flushed red.
'Flore Pleno' – double white flowers.

0.4 × 0.8   E or B   Sun or shade

IRIS
A very important group of perennials with sword- or grass-like leaves and the famous 'flag' type flower. The following species (and their varieties) are the best for bog and water-side planting and are readily obtainable:
I. chrysographes – refined yet striking; flowers range in colour from white and blue shades to dark velvety violet and almost black – but all are prettily marked with gold.
I. ensata – a superb iris native of Japan with flattened or drooping falls to the flowers that range in colour from red-purple to lilac. Plant in acid soil out of water but near enough

Hosta fortunei var. *albopicta*

Houttuynia cordata

Iris ensata (cultivar)

Ligularia przewalskii

for the roots to reach it. It is still sold under its old name, *I. kaempferi*.

I. laevigata – grows well actually in water. It has brilliant blue flowers in June and July but there are white and bi-coloured forms and an excellent variegated-leaf form. Neat and non-invasive, excellent for small ponds.

I. pseudacorus, yellow flag – our native iris which is ideal for a wildlife pond and will seed itself around; there is a good variegated leaf form.

I. sibirica – grassy leaves and many different flower colours (including red, purple, plum, blues and whites). Excellent for naturalizing large areas.

I. versicolor – short with blue flowers. The variety 'Kermesina' has beautiful claret flowers; prefers sun.

0.2 to 1.0 × 0.3 to 0.6   E or B   Sun or part shade

JUNCUS RUSH
Hairless perennials with leaves rounded in cross-section which, unlike grasses and sedges, have recognizable small green, brown or yellowish flowers in June or July. Although not wildly decorative, many such as the soft rush (*J. effusus*) and the hard rush (*J. inflexus*) are common British natives and are suitable for the wildlife pond or lake where loose stands in shallow water provide cover for aquatic animals and fish that like to spawn among them.

1.0 × 1.0   E or B   Sun or part shade

KIRENGESHOMA PALMATA
A Japanese gem of a perennial with broad angled leaves and, in early autumn, delicate sprays of creamy-yellow flowers like miniature shuttlecocks. It likes a rich, deep moist soil and cool air. Difficult to find, but worth the effort.

0.9 × 0.6   E   Shade or cool sun

LAGAROSIPHON MAJOR CURLY WATER THYME

Often sold under the name *Elodea crispa*, this South African native with narrow brittle curled leaves is a good oxygenator for any size of pond. It is normally sold in small bunches held together by a lead weight that you just throw into your pond. It may be damaged in severe winters. Beware of *Elodea canadensis*, the Canadian pondweed, which is too rampant for anything but lakes. Like most oxygenating plants *Lagarosiphon* will also provide shelter for fish fry and other small water creatures.

– × 1.5   O   Sun

LIGULARIA

A genus of large perennials needing moist or boggy conditions, they are grown for their bold foliage and their tall spikes or branching heads of orange or yellow daisy-like flowers. The following types are readily available:

L. dentata 'Desdemona' – more compact than most, so suitable for the smaller pond. Large rounded leaves brownish-green above and purple-red underneath; orange flowers in late summer.

L. 'Gregynog Gold' – heart-shaped leaves and large spikes of orange flowers; a large plant.

L. przewalskii – fringed leaves and large spikes of yellow flowers.

1.0 to 2.0 × 1.0 to 1.5   E or B   Some sun or shade

LOBELIA

The dimensions below relate to a number of species that are erect perennials requiring rich, moist soils and look nothing like the bedding lobelia.

L. cardinalis – brilliant scarlet flowers.

L. × *gerardii* 'Verdrariensis' – purple flowers.

L. siphilitica – blue flowers; likes wet clay.

L. × *speciosa* – scarlet, crimson, pink or magenta flowers and dark foliage.

0.9 × 0.3   E or B   Sun

LYSICHITON BOG ARUM
An extraordinary genus commonly represented by two species. Both have squat arum-like flowers appearing with the emerging leaves in early spring. As the season progresses, the leaves take over – in a big way.
L. americanus – the larger of the two and more often seen. It has yellow, unpleasantly-scented flowers and large surf-board shaped leaves (up to 1.2 m long).
L. camtschatcensis – white flowers, sweetly scented and smaller leaves.

    0.9 to 1.2 X 1.0 to 1.5   E or B   Sun or part shade
....

LYSIMACHIA LOOSESTRIFE
L. vulgaris is our native yellow loosestrife. Although invasive it is suitable for a wildlife pond. The yellow flower spikes appear in summer. *L. punctata* is a prettier, close relative from South-east Europe, but is similarly invasive and needs plenty of room. *L. nummularia* is completely different. It has a low creeping habit (0.1 × 1.0), hence the common name, creeping Jenny. It has rounded leaves and yellow bell-like flowers. It loves damp shade and is suitable for the edges of small ponds. It is normally seen in its attractive gold-leaved variety, 'Aurea'.

    0.9 × 0.3   E or B   Sun or shade
....

LYTHRUM SALICARIA PURPLE LOOSESTRIFE
A native perennial with tall spikes of bright pink flowers in mid to late summer and fine foliage tints in autumn. Selected varieties include 'Firecandle' and 'The Beacon' which are deeper in flower colour.

    1.2 × 0.5   E or B   Sun or part shade
....

MATTEUCCIA STRUTHIOPTERIS OSTRICH PLUME FERN
A very pretty hardy perennial fern with a shuttlecock arrangement of dainty fronds that are especially attractive in

Lobelia cardinalis

Lysichiton americanus

Lysimachia punctata

Matteuccia struthiopteris

Menyanthes trifoliata

Mimulus cupreus 'Whitecroft Scarlet'

spring when they have a translucent quality. It is somewhat apt to creep about.

1.0 × 0.6   E or B   Shade

....

MENYANTHES TRIFOLIATA BOG BEAN
A deciduous perennial with three-parted leaves like those of broad beans and a short spike of beautiful pink and white flowers fringed with long white hairs in May and June. A pretty native of shallow fresh water, marshes and fens and a food plant of elephant hawk-moth larvae.

0.2 × 1.0   M   Sun

....

MIMULUS MONKEY MUSK
Rampant perennials native of the Americas with brightly-coloured red, orange and yellow variously spotted flowers in summer that look like chubby snapdragons. *M. moschatus* and *M. guttatus*, both with yellow flowers, are pretty plants but are

Myosotis scorpiodes

considered by some to be a real menace. They rapidly spread
by seeding themselves around and smother or choke other
plants. In a large water garden this is less of a problem and
may even be desirable. *M. luteus* is much safer with red-brown
blotches on the yellow petals; it has the strange common
name blood-drop emlets. Others include:

M. cardinalis – scarlet, red and yellow forms.

M. lewisii – pink or red flowers.

M. ringens – bluish-mauve flowers.

There are also a number of named hybrids including a strain
often sold as a bedding plant (Queen's Prize) which offers
good value.

0.6 to 1.0 × 0.6   E or B   Sun

MYOSOTIS SCORPIOIDES WATER FORGET-ME-NOT
A charming native perennial with typical blue forget-me-not
flowers from June onwards. It spreads rather fast so in a small

water garden choose the more compact 'Mermaid' which also
has larger and longer-lasting flowers.

0.25 × 0.6   E or B   Sun or part shade

MYRICA

M. gale is our native bog myrtle, a compact deciduous shrub
that grows in acidic bogs and has golden-brown catkins and
sweetly-scented foliage. *M. californica* is the Californian
bayberry, a large evergreen shrub with glistening evergreen
foliage and dark purple fruit that persists into winter; it too is
suitable for wet, acidic soils.

0.5 to 1.5 × 0.5 to 1.5   E   Sun

MYRIOPHYLLUM AQUATICUM PARROT'S FEATHER

An underwater perennial that occasionally peeps above water.
The foliage is blue-green and very feathery. It supplies oxygen
to the water and is ideal for providing cover and protection
for fish and other pond-life as well as being good at hiding
unsightly edges of pools. It is slightly tender which helps keep
it under control but it rarely dies off completely. It is easily
reduced by pulling out. *M. spicatum* is the native spiked water
milfoil which is suitable only for large natural wildlife ponds.
M. verticillatum is the whorled water milfoil. It has greenish-
yellow foliage and again is too rampant for smaller ponds.

– 2.0   O   Sun

NYMPHAEA WATER-LILY

One of the most decorative of all cultivated plants – in or out
of water – much loved by gardeners all over the world for
thousands of years. Technically, they are deciduous, summer
flowering, perennial water plants with floating, usually
rounded leaves and perfectly formed, brightly coloured flowers that also sit on the water surface. They vary from fully
hardy to frost tender and require full sun, some soil in the
bottom of the pond (or in a container) to root into and prefer

Myriophyllum aquaticum

Nymphaea 'Mme Wilfon Gonnère'

Nymphaea 'Laydekeri Fulgens'

Orontium aquaticum

Osmunda regalis

still water. They vary in size and vigour from slow miniatures (that will grow in very small shallow ponds, even just a half oak barrel) to very vigorous species that require a large lake. They spread by tuber-like rhizomes which need dividing and replanting in spring every 3 to 5 years. See the Checklist for details of varieties.

– 1.0 to 6.0   F   Sun

NYMPHOIDES PELTATA WATER FRINGE
A deciduous perennial with floating, waterlily-like leaves and fringed yellow flowers in late summer. A rampant native needing space.

0.2 × 1.5   F   Sun

ORONTIUM AQUATICUM GOLDEN CLUB
An excellent perennial aquatic plant with a strange yellow and white flower that is a spadix (without a spathe) in May, bizarrely described as resembling 'white worms with yellow heads trying to take off'. The oblong leaves have a waxy coating which makes them unwettable.

0.2 × 1.0   M or F   Sun

OSMUNDA REGALIS ROYAL FERN
A large, handsome fern with brown tinted leaves in spring and autumn. It needs plenty of room and prefers an acidic soil. *O.r.* var. *gracilis* is a smaller form with copper-coloured young fronds.

1.2 × 1.0   B or E   Sun or shade

POLYGONUM KNOTWEED
These tough, vigorous perennials are very variable. Those that like wet conditions are:
P. affine – a low spreading carpeter with small white to crimson flower spikes in late summer and early autumn; 'Superbum' is a good form with fine autumn tints (0.3 × 0.6).

P. amplexicaule – a tall perennial with rich crimson flower spikes in late summer, especially in the variety 'Atrosanguineum' (1.2 × 1.2).

P. bistorta – a strong perennial, excellent en masse, with pink flowers in early summer; 'Superbum' is the form of this native usually available (0.8 × 0.8).

P. milletii – narrow leaves and long-lasting crimson flowers (0.6 × 0.6).

0.3 to 1.2 × 0.6 to 1.2   B or E   Sun or part shade

PRIMULA

A massive genus of perennials, many of which prefer moist conditions. Most flower in spring or early summer. The flower colours are very diverse including both pastel and 'hot' shades. *P. denticulata*, the drumstick primula, and *P. rosea* are small in stature; others are taller and can be grouped under the term 'Candelabra', which describes the whorled arrangement of flowers up the stems. These include *P. pulverulenta, P. japonica, P. prolifera, P. bulleyana, P. beesiana, P. sikkimensis* and many hybrids. *P. florindae* is the giant of the genus, reaching well over one metre.

0.1 to 0.9 × 0.10 to 0.3   B or E   Some sun or shade

RHEUM PALMATUM   ORNAMENTAL RHUBARB

Imposing perennials with huge maple-like leaves and lofty spikes of cream flowers in early summer. The variety 'Atrosanguineum' has red flowers and reddish undersides to the leaves. An excellent waterside plant for medium to large ponds.

1.6 × 1.4   E   Sun or shade

RODGERSIA

Perennials worth growing as much for their foliage as their summer flowers.

R. aesculifolia – chestnut-like leaves and creamy-white or pink flowers on pyramidal spikes.

Primula japonica

R. pinnata – fingered leaves and pink flowers. Seek out the form 'Superba' with bronzy leaves and deep rose flowers.

R. podophylla – lobed leaves and buff-coloured flowers.

R. tabularis – now known as *Astilboides tabularis*, it has huge circular leaves with the leaf stalk attached to the middle of it (like an umbrella blown inside-out) and creamy-white flowers.

0.9 to 1.2 × 0.6 to 0.9   E   Sun or partial shade

SAGITTARIA SAGITTIFOLIA ARROWHEAD
Handsome arrow-shaped leaves and, in summer, spikes of white, three-petalled flowers with dark centres. A native of flowing, shallow water. There is a double-flowered variety.

0.10 × 1.0   M   Sun

SALIX WILLOW
A large group of deciduous shrubs, scrubby medium or large trees with catkin flowers, many of which are British natives and all do well in a wet, waterside position. Good examples include:
S. alba var. *sericea* – a small tree with silver foliage; can be stooled (cut back hard every spring).
S. babylonica var *pekinensis* 'Tortuosa' – a vigorous form with twisted and contorted branches.
S. caprea, goat willow – a common native with yellow 'pussy' catkins in spring; for the wildlife water garden.
S. × sepulcralis 'Chrysocoma' – the ubiquitous weeping willow of the sides of village ponds and parkland lakes. Avoid planting near buildings in heavy clay soils.

1.5 to 15.0 × 1.5 to 8.0   E   Sun

SCIRPUS RUSH
Despite the common name, these are perennial sedge grasses, *S. lacustris* being the native common club rush. For the decorative water garden choose the zebra rush (don't be put off by its long Latin name, *Scirpus lacustris* subsp. *tabernaemontani* 'Zebrinus'), a very beautiful plant with white horizontal striping to the stems.

1.0 to 1.5 × 0.5 to 1.0   E or B   Sun

SPARTINA PECTINATA PRAIRIE CORD GRASS
A vigorous invasive grass. The clone 'Aureomarginata' has ribbon-like yellow-striped leaves and attractive green and purple flowers.

1.5 × 0.9   E or B   Sun

Rheum palmatum

Rodgersia podophylla

Spartina pectinata 'Aureomarginata'

Stratiotes aloïdes

STRATIOTES ALOIDES WATER SOLDIER

Semi-evergreen perennial with narrow, spiny leaves arranged in rosettes. The flowers are small, globular and white and appear in summer. Needs regular control.

0.2 × 0.3   F   Sun

TYPHA REED MACE

Well known grass-like plants with brown poker-like heads that are wrongly called bullrushes. The common species are of varying stature which governs the size of pond they suit.

T. minima – a dainty species (0.4 m tall) suitable for medium sized ponds; flowerheads are like velvet drumsticks.

T. laxmannii – middle-sized species (1.0 m tall) suitable for slightly larger ponds.

T. angustifolia – graceful but large (2.0 m tall) suitable for large ponds.

Typha minima

Zantedeshia aethiopica

T. latifolia – the one to avoid: very big (3.0 m) and does not stop spreading, forming mats of roots that can clog even large areas of water.

0.4 to 2.0 × 1.0 to 3.0   B or M   Sun

ZANTEDESCHIA AETHIOPICA   ARUM LILY
A superb perennial for the highly ornamental water garden. Large white spathes all summer and dark, glossy, spear-shaped foliage. Better in deeper rather than shallow water in colder regions so that the roots are below the freezing line. 'Crowborough' is hardier (once established) and more tolerant of drier conditions.

1.0 × 0.6   B or M   Sun or part shade

PLANT CHECKLISTS

A FINGERTIP GUIDE TO PLANTS FOR A WATER GARDEN

PLANTS FOR THE WILDLIFE WATER AND BOG GARDEN

These plants are a selection of attractive native, naturalized or exotic species that offer good shelter and breeding sites for the pondlife community.

Ajuga reptans Bugle B
Angelica sylvestris Angelica MB
Butomus umbellatus Flowering Rush M
Callitriche stagnalis Water Starwort O
Caltha palustris Marsh Marigold MB
Cardamine pratensis Lady's Smock MB
Carex Sedge (some invasive) MB
Ceratophyllum demersum Hornwort FO
Cornus alba Red-barked Dogwood E
Cyperus longus Galingale (invasive) M
Epilobium hirsutum Greater Willowherb (invasive) B

Eupatorium cannabinum Hemp Agrimony B
Filipendula ulmaria Meadowsweet B
Fritillaria meleagris Snake's-head Fritillary B
Geum rivale Water Avens B
Hottonia palustris Water Violet F
Hydrocharis morsus-ranae Frogbit F
Iris pseudacorus Yellow Iris MB
Lychnis flos-cuculi Ragged-Robin B
Lycopus europaeus Gipsywort M
Lysimachia nemorum Wood Pimpernel B
Lysimachia vulgaris Yellow Loosestrife M
Lythrum salicaria Purple Loosestrife MB
Mentha aquatica Water mint (invasive) M
Menyanthes trifoliata Bogbean M
Mimulus guttatus Monkeyflower – (invasive) M
Myosotis scorpioides Water Forget-me-not MB
Myriophyllum spicatum Spiked water-milfoil O

Nymphaea Water-lily F
Nymphoides peltata Water Fringe
(invasive) F
Osmunda regalis Royal Fern B
Polygonum amphibium Amphibious
Bistort M
Primula Candelabra types B
Ranunculus lingua Greater
Spearwort M
Ranunculus Water-Crowfoot F
Sagittaria sagittifolia Arrowhead M
Salix Willow E
Typha Reed Mace (some invasive)
M
Veronica beccabunga Brooklime M
Viburnum opulus Guelder Rose E

Key
E – Water's edge plant tolerating
moist conditions.
B – Bog or shallow marginal plant
(0 to 5 cm)
M Deep marginal plant
(5 to 30 cm)
F – Floating or deep water aquatic
O – Oxygenating, submerged
aquatic

**BOG OR SHALLOW MARGINAL
PLANTS (0 TO 5 CM OF WATER)**

(designated 'B' in Directory)

Aconitum Monkshood
Acorus gramineus
Alisma Water Plantain
Astilbe
Butomus umbellatus Flowering Rush
Calla palustris Bog Arum
Caltha palustris Marsh Marigold,
Kingcup
Carex Sedge

Cotula cornopifolia Golden Buttons
Darmera peltata Umbrella Plant
Eleocharis acicularis Hair grass
Eriophorum angustifolium Cotton
Grass
Filipendula Meadowsweet
Geum rivale Water Avens
Glyceria maxima Reed Sweet Grass
Gunnera manicata Prickly Rhubarb
Hemerocallis Day lily
Houttuynia cordata
Iris (see Directory)
Juncus Rush
Ligularia
Lobelia
Lychnis flos-cuculi Ragged Robin
Lysichiton Bog Arum
Lysimachia Loosestrife
Lythrum saliarica Purple
Loosestrife
Matteuccia struthiopteris Ostrich
Plume Fern
Mentha aquatica Water Mint
Mimulus Monkey Musk
Mysotis scorpioides Water Forget-
me-not
Onoclea sensibilis Sensitive Fern
Osmunda regalis Royal Fern
Peltandra undulata Arrow Arum
Polygonum Knotweed
Pontederia cordata Pickerel Weed
Primula
Ranunculus Spearwort
Sagittaria sagittifolia Arrowhead
Saururus cernuus Lizard's Tail
Scirpus Rush
Scrophularia aquatica Figwort
Spartina pectinata Prairie Cord Grass
Typha Reed Mace
Veronica beccabunga Brooklime
Zantedeschia aethiopica Arum Lily

WATER'S EDGE PLANTS

(designated 'E' in Directory)

Perennials

Aconitum Monkshood
Acorus calamus Sweet Flag
Actaea Baneberry
Ajuga reptans Bugle
Alchemilla mollis Lady's Mantle
Arum italicum Lords and Ladies
Aruncus dioicus Goat's Beard
Astilbe
Astilboides tabularis
Astrantia Masterwort
Brunnera macrophylla Perennial
  Forget-me-not
Buphthalmum salicifolium Oxeye
Cimicifuga Bugbane
Darmera peltata Umbrella Plant
Dicentra Bleeding Heart
Euphorbia palustris Spurge
Filipendula Meadowsweet
Gentiana asclepiadea Willow
  Gentian
Gentiana pneumonanthe Marsh
  Gentian
Geranium Crane's-bill
Geum rivale Water Avens
Gunnera manicata Prickly Rhubarb
Hemerocallis Daylily
Hosta Plantain Lily, Giboshi
Houttuynia cordata
Iris
Kirengeshoma palmata
Ligularia
Lobelia
Lysichiton Bog Arum
Lysimachia Loosestrife
Lythrum salicaria Purple
  Loosestrife

Iris pseudacorus

Meconopsis
Mimulus Monkey Musk
Monarda didyma Bergamot
Myosotis scorpioides Water Forget-
  me-not
Osmunda regalis Royal Fern
Polygonum Knotweed
Primula
Ranunculus Buttercup
Rheum palmatum Ornamental
  Rhubarb
Rodgersia
Scrophularia aquatica Figwort
Smilacina racemosa False Spikenard
Thalictrum Meadow Rue

Tricyrtis hirta Toad Lily
Trillium Wake Robin
Trollius Globeflower
Uvularia Merry-bells
Veratrum False Helleborine

Bulbs

Camassia
Cardiocrinum giganteum Giant Lily
Fritillara meleagris Snake's-head Fritillary
Leucojum Snowflake
Lilium canadense Canadian Lily
L. pardalinum Leopard Lily
L. superbum Swamp Lily
Schizostylis coccinea Kaffir Lily

Grasses, Sedges and Rushes

Alopecurus pratensis Meadow Foxtail Grass
Carex
Deschampsia cespitosa Tufted Hair Grass
Glyceria maxima
Hakonechloa
Holcus mollis Yorkshire Fog
Juncus
Milium effusum 'Aureum' Bowles' Golden Grass
Miscanthus
Phalaris arundinacea
Scirpus
Spartina pectinata Prairie Cord Grass

Many species of bamboos will also tolerate moist conditions.

Ferns

Athyrium filix-femina Lady Fern
Onoclea sensibilis Sensitive Fern

Polystichum setiferum Soft Shield Fern
Woodwardia
Matteuccia struthiopteris Ostrich Plume Fern

FLOATING AQUATICS

(designated 'F' in Directory)

Aponogeton distachyos Cape Pondweed, Water Hawthorn
Azolla caroliniana Fairy Moss, Water Fern
Eichhornia crassipes Water Hyacinth
Hydrocharis morsus-ranae Frogbit
Nymphaea Water-lily
Nymphoides peltata Water Fringe
Orontium aquaticum Golden Club
Pistia stratiotes Water Lettuce
Stratiotes aloides Water Soldier
Trapa natans Water Chestnut

OXYGENATING, SUBMERGED AQUATIC PLANTS

(designated 'O' in Directory)

Callitriche Water starwort
Ceratophyllum demersum Hornwort
Crasula recurva
Eleocharis Hair Grass, Spike Rush
Fontinalis antipyretica Willow Moss
Hottonia palustris Water Violet
Lagarosiphon major Curly Water Thyme
Myriophyllum aquaticum Parrot's Feather (and others)
Potamogeton Pondweed (invasive)
Ranunculus Water Crowfoot

WATER-LILIES

There are hundreds of varieties of water-lilies. The list of readily available types breaks down the genus by vigour and thus their suitability for different sized water gardens. Always keep a look out for new varieties: there are some excellent recent additions from America.

For tubs and/or very shallow water (15 cm deep)

N. 'Aurora' – yellow flowers
N. × *helvola* (*N. pygmaea* 'Helvola') – yellow flowers
N. 'Laydekeri Lilacea' – pink flowers
N. 'Odorata Minor' – white flowers
N. 'Pygmaea Rubis' – red flowers
N. tetragona (*N. pygmaea* 'Alba') – white flowers

For small ponds (15 – 60 cm deep)

N. candida – white flowers
N. caroliniana 'Rosea' (*N. caroliniana*) – pink flowers
N. 'Ellisiana' – red flowers
N. 'Firecrest' – pink flowers
N. 'Froebelii' – red flowers
N. 'Gonnère – white flowers
N. 'Hermine' – white flowers
N. 'Laydekeri Fulgens' – red flowers
N. odorata (*N.* 'Odorata Alba') – white flowers
N. 'Odorata Sulphurea Grandiflora' – yellow flowers

N. 'Odorata Turicensis' – pink flowers
N. 'Paul Hariot' – yellow flowers
N. 'Pink Opal' – red flowers
N. 'Solfatare' – yellow flowers

For medium ponds (30 – 90 cm deep)

N. 'Albatros' – white flowers
N. 'Comanche' – yellow flowers
N. 'James Brydon' – red flowers
N. 'Marliacea Albida' – white flowers
N. 'Marliacea Rosea' – pink flowers
N. 'Marliacea Rubra Punctata' – red flowers
N. 'Moorei' – yellow flowers
N. 'Mrs. Richmond' – pink flowers
N. 'Pink Sensation' – pink flowers
N. 'René Gérard' – red flowers
N. 'Rose Arey' – pink flowers
N. 'Rosennymphe' – red flowers
N. 'Sioux' – yellow flowers

For medium to large ponds (0.8 to 1.2 deep)

N. 'Attraction' – red flowers
N. 'Escarboucle' – red flowers
N. 'Marliacea Carnea' – pink flowers
N. 'Marliacea Chromatella' – yellow flowers
N. 'Masaniello' – pink flowers
N. 'Rembrandt' – red flowers
N. 'Sirius' – red flowers
N. 'Sunrise' – yellow flowers
N. tuberosa 'Alba' – white flowers
N. tuberosa 'Richardsonii' – white flowers

Vigorous and invasive types for large ponds and lakes

N. 'Charles de Meurville' – red flowers
N. 'Colonel A.J. Welch' – yellow flowers
N. 'Colossea' – pink flowers
N. 'Conqueror' – red flowers

N. 'Gladstoneana' – white flowers
N. 'Norma Gedye' – pink flowers
N. alba – white flowers
N. tuberosa 'Rosea' – red flowers

Note: The naming of water-lilies is in a confused state. The names in brackets are synonyms that are still in use.

TREES, SHRUBS AND CONIFERS TOLERATING WATERSIDE CONDITIONS

Acer rubrum Red Maple
Alnus Alder
Andromeda polifolia Bog Rosemary
Arctostaphylos Bearberry
Betula nigra River Birch
Betula pubescens Downy birch
Clethra alnifolia Sweet Pepper Bush
Cornus Dogwood
Gaultheria procumbens Creeping Wintergreen
Kalmia latifolia Calico Bush
Liquidambar styraciflua Sweet Gum
Metasequoia glyptostroboides Dawn Redwood
Myrica Bog Myrtle, Bayberry
Populus Poplar
Salix Willow
Sorbaria
Taxodium distichum Swamp Cypress
Vaccinium Blueberry
Viburnum opulus Guelder Rose

VIGOROUS AND INVASIVE WATER AND BOG PLANTS UNSUITABLE FOR SMALL AND MEDIUM SIZED PONDS

Carex pseudocyperus Cyperus Sedge
Carex riparia Great Pond Sedge
Cyperus longus Galingale
Elodea canadensis Canadian Pondweed
Epilobium hirsutum Greater Willowherb
Heracleum mantegazzianum Giant Hogweed

Hippuris vulgaris Marestail
Juncus effusus Soft Rush
Lemna Duckweed
Mentha aquatica Water Mint
Mimulus guttatus Monkey Flower
Nuphar lutea Yellow Water-lily
Nymphaea alba Water-lily
Nymphoides peltata Water fringe
Phragmites communis Norfolk Reed
Polygonum cuspidatum Japanese knotweed
Potamogeton Pondweed
Scutellaria galericulata Skullcap
Sparganium Bur-reed
Typha latifolia Reed Mace
Zizania latifolia Canadian Wild Rice

Typha latifolia

Useful Addresses

Most garden centres, plant centres and nurseries offer a wide range of
suitable plants and equipment, but the following companies supply some
of the more specialized products:

Anglo Aquarium Plant Company (pools, fountains, plants and fish),
Wayside, Cattlegate Road, Enfield, Middlesex EN2 9DP

Bennett's Water Lily Farm (plants),
Putton Lane, Chickerell, Weymouth, Dorset DT3 4AF

Dunlop Limited (pool liners), GRG Division,
Pimbo Industrial Estate, Skelmersdale, Lancashire

Honeysome Aquatic Nursery (plants),
The Row, Sutton, Cambridgeshire, CB6 2PF

Lotus Water Garden Products (pools, fountains, plants and fish),
260–300 Berkhampstead Road, Chesham, Buckinghamshire HP5 3EY

Nightscaping (garden and pond lighting),
352 Old York Road, London SW18 15S

Stapeley Water Gardens Ltd (plants),
Stapeley, Nantwich, Cheshire CW5 7LH

H. Tisbury and Sons (plants),
Spice Pitts Farm, Church Road., Noak Hill, Romford, Essex

The Water Garden Nursery (plants),
Highcroft, Moorend, Wembworthy, Chulmleigh, Devon EX18 7SG

Westcountry Water Garden Centre (plants),
Burston Bow, Crediton, Devon EX17 6LB

Wildwoods Water Gardens (plants),
Theobalds Park Road, Crews Hill, Enfield, Middlesex,EN2 9BP

PICTURE ACKNOWLEDGEMENTS

b–bottom/c–centre/l–left/r–right/t–top
Eric Crichton 7, 27, 29 (tr & br), 30, 33, 36 (t), 39 (t & bl),
43 (tl & br), 44, 48 (t & bl)
Jerry Harpur 1, 6 (designer M. Balston), 21, 23 (Shute House)
Andrew Lawson 5 (t), 29 (tl & bl), 31 (r), 32, 35 (l), 39 (br), 43 (b & c),
45, 47 (b), 48 (br), 51, 53 (t & bl), 58
S. & O. Mathews front cover inset, 25, 31 (l), 35 (r)
National Trust/Mike Williams front cover background, 61
Clive Nichols back cover, 8, 14, 36 (b), 43 (tr), 55
Oxford Scientific Films / H. Taylor 56
Photos Horticultural 47 (t), 53 (br), 54, 62
Harry Smith Collection 14
Spanish Tourist Office / A. Garrido 5 (b)
John Woodcock 13